STAKING
Your Life

What Drives *Your* Beliefs?

Dan Lemburg

CommuningWithGod.org

Scripture quotations are taken from The Holy Bible, English
Standard Version (ESV), copyright 2001 by Crossway, a publishing
ministry of Good News Publishers. All rights reserved.

ISBN 979-8-218-71472-7

Contents Herein

Why?

L et's begin at the heart of the matter: *Why am I here?* Surely you have thought about this at one time or another; perhaps it preoccupies you! Why *are* you here? Obviously, we are talking about a whole lot more than just your physical locale. What we're about to discuss is the *meaning of life*.

The sheer ability of human consciousness, this vital gift of awareness, enables us to interact with our world and the people in it, thus bringing us a genuine sense of personal meaning—a justification of sorts for our existence. So, is it about who you may be as to your family relationships: a spouse, a parent, a son or a daughter, or in regard to the significance you may find in your many other interpersonal connections? Yes, these all do bring meaning, but is this the intention for your life, the sum of it?

And then there's the issue of personal accomplishment: are you merely here to do a job, to make a difference in this world you've been birthed into—to bring happiness to those around you, or at the other end of the spectrum, to selfishly pursue all the fulfillment you can possibly muster during the brief time you've been allotted? Is your purpose about pleasure; about prestige?

Okay, let's say you've accomplished all that. Then what? More and more frequently I hear the mantra of a materialistic world view: "Well, when it's all over, I simply cease to exist. And that's why I need to grab everything I can right now to somehow experience every ounce of personal pleasure and fulfillment before I exit. After all, It's *my* life!" This is the *Secular Humanist* view of life; it is materialistic in nature. "What you see is what you get. Get used to it, brother—ain't nothin' else! No soul, no spirit, certainly no God and consequently no hereafter as the religious would have you believe." Yet, if the aphorism "there are no atheists in foxholes" is true, this position has a whole lot of holes in it! Just what do we in fact believe about our existence? And why is the truth about it important?

There are also those who believe in God, who are convinced that we possess an eternal soul, although somewhat blindly so, and are reasonably confident there is life after this one has passed. These comprise a much larger group, but are often just as materialistic: "Sure, I believe in God, and I'm pretty sure I'm going to heaven. After all, I've been a fairly good person." These folks never really dig into the meaning of life; they merely take it as it comes, not giving much attention as to the *why* of things. Will they one day actually experience what they've been taking for granted—heaven as they have pictured it? Or will they be disappointed in life's ultimate outcome?

To be clear, we are talking about people here, some good and some not so good, but in the end people—just people—all striving to maintain life where they find themselves planted. And there are billions of us—more and more all the time—all, consciously or subconsciously asking, "Why?" This book is not meant to be a court of condemnation for any particular individual or group; it's merely an investigation.

Does God actually exist? And if so, what is my responsibility toward him, or *it* as some suppose. Is he an all-powerful and all-knowing personal deity, or some sort of cosmic force possessing an attribute of supreme intelligence capable of presiding over the universe? What if there truly is more to life than I thought, a greater purpose for my life than I assumed—more accountability here and now? "I certainly don't want to be caught with my pants down! Maybe I should have looked into this a little more seriously."

A myriad of questions surround this issue. But why all the mystery? If there actually is a God, why doesn't he just present himself in a way that leaves no room for doubt? Why am I being asked to believe in something I can't see, or experience with any of my other physical senses? How can I be held liable for something so ethereal?

WHY? is ultimately the question. What purpose is there in it all? Now that's precisely the relevant question: our discussion needs to be centered on the question of purpose—though not our purpose, but God's. And despite the mystery, his purpose for us and the world we inhabit can be discovered. That is, if we look in the right places. So, if all this is true, there must be a relevant source for information, a starting place. Is it possible that the Bible—being of ancient origin—actually provides a plausible explanation?

Origins

"In the beginning…" Where does one begin? As I look up into the vastness of the night sky, I can't help but wonder how the enormity of what is spread out before us all came about. Think about it for a moment! We are talking about a universe unimaginable in scope. The observable universe is about 95 billion light-years from end to end, and encompasses at least two trillion galaxies, each containing a couple billion stars. More than that, the universe we are unable to observe is thought to be 250 times as large. Given that light travels at 670,616,629 miles per hour and there are 8,760 hours in a year (the definition of a *light year*), how can we fathom it all? We can't—we simply can't! What we see *up there* lies beyond human comprehension.

A little perspective might help here. Apart from science fiction, our current aspiration of manned space flight is realistically limited to the idea of reaching our closest neighbor, Mars—a mere 140 million miles away. Yet even this tiny jump pushes the boundaries of our technical ability. We are indeed a mere blip in this incredible cosmos.

Why does it exist? In Genesis 1:1, the Bible tells us that God is behind it all: "In the beginning God created the heavens and the earth." John 1:3 says that all things came into being through Jesus Christ; he is its author. Colossians 1:16 further explains, "…all things have been created through Him and for Him." But again, *why*? Why would God, the self-existent and self-sufficient One bother? Why put himself through all the effort it took—and evidently takes—to create and sustain it? What is his *purpose* in it all? Well, this is the very reason for this book: not necessarily to provide a detailed explanation, but to at least ponder what might be the motives behind God's mind-blowing plan.

Origins is our theme for the moment. As scientists look into the reason behind our being, a startling reality has come to light. We find that our existence would not be possible without the cosmos having been fine-tuned to accommodate life. Here we are, spinning through space on this speck of a planet. Look around you. Think about the habitable belt encasing the earth enabling life we so often take for granted: the sunlight, the water, the atmosphere, the land—all here to provide a home for vegetation and animals, not the least of which for creatures like you and me. None of it would be possible if the cosmos had not been fine-tuned for this very purpose.

Without this star we call the Sun being its precise size and composition, and Earth positioned precisely in proximity to the sun, life as we know it would not be possible. Any closer and we would fry, and further away and we would freeze. Additionally, chemical elements emanating from the sun provide the components essential to life. Both Earth's size and its molten core generate a magnetic field shielding us from the sun's deadly radiation (the solar wind) which otherwise would have stripped away our atmosphere long ago. Earth's rotation causing day and night, and seasons brought on by earth's tilt on its axis as it travels around the sun, are critical to life's existence.

Our moon, unique in size among others in our solar system, fits us perfectly; its gravitational field and rotation around Earth causes not only essential ocean tides, but also brings a stabilizing effect without which our planet would tend to wobble, disrupting seasons. Even the outer planets of our solar system bring welcome protection, the massive gravitational force of their utter size drawing away asteroids which would certainly doom us if allowed to wander into our sphere.

Fine-tuned? Undeniable! While I am merely capable of presenting a somewhat crude summary of the physics surrounding us, it merely scratches the surface of the detailed information now at our disposal. Awe-inspiring evidence is there for the asking should one want to delve further into the subject. And we've not yet begun to explore the questions surrounding life itself. We'll talk about that next.

Purpose

As we touched on earlier, Secularists—of whom much of western humanity is comprised—believe that there is little or no meaning to everything. We live, we die, and that's the sum of it. In their view, nothing lies beyond physical death. We simply cease to exist. Chaos is the watchword for their worldview. Why does the wonder of planet Earth provide a home to live out our short lives? "Don't know; just randomly all came together, I guess. But since we're here, let's make the best of it by trying to experience as much personal pleasure and accomplishment—purpose, so to speak—to this otherwise meaningless existence."

On the other hand, might there actually be a sense of order to what these folks perceive as an unplanned reality? There is indeed an open secret to be dealt with. The first chapter of the Book of Romans describes a world of order, a world where the splendor and beauty of our planetary home is meant to lead us to the brilliant God who created it. Verse 20 declares, "For since the creation of the world His invisible attributes, His eternal power and divine nature, have been clearly seen, being understood through what has been made, so that they are without excuse." According to this passage of the Bible, at bare minimum mankind appears to be held accountable to take it a step further—to explore our earthly reality and the God who is behind it all.

Beginnings? Evolution has been submitted as the reason for life as we know it. Given this view, all life originated from a single-cell organism brought into being through natural processes sometime in earth's distant past. Didn't life have to start somewhere? Although this model remains a theory, it is widely accepted and taught as fact across the spectrum of society. Those, in fact, who hold to any other view are commonly regarded as incompetent Cretans. But while there is substance to the idea of species nominally mutating over time through adaptation to their environment, what is often swept under the rug is the literal *Origin of Life* itself. Just how did that single-cell organism (from which all life supposedly evolved) come into being: how and when did that life first appear?

After many decades of research into this question, science continues to be baffled. There simply is no explanation as to how that first cell, which we now know to be complex way beyond what it was first imagined to be, was first constructed from inorganic chemicals thought to have been prevalent in the primeval world. In actual fact, the chance of that ever happening is infinitesimally remote.

First, the molecular components of that cell would need to come together in exactly the right order for it to function a "living" organism. What is meant by a *living organism*? Metabolism is the essential element. The dictionary defines *metabolism* as: "The chemical changes in living cells by which energy is provided for vital processes and activities and new material." The complexity of these processes cannot be overstated. Where would the information needed to achieve this wonder come from?

Next, the single-cell organism must be able both to protect itself from degeneration and then somehow replicate itself. How likely do you think it might be for such an organism to first possess these qualities and then maintain them in a hostile environment, even if it somehow randomly came into existence? Zero!

Science explains that given infinite time to work with, this could possibly have happened naturally. Yet, the problem is that given the odds, since the universe is generally accepted as being approximately 13.8 billion years old, there simply is not enough time, mathematically, for their theory even to be considered as a viable explanation.

For these irrefutable reasons science justifiably remains mystified. Those science shows on TV never bother to explain what they allege to be true—life springing from some primordial soup. They assume no one would ask, no doubt. Since there in fact remains no viable answer for life launching naturally, their theory of its origin *must* be held as a presupposition. Those who stubbornly cling to the secular materialist view of life need to have some sort of rational footing! Otherwise, how could they reasonably reject the existence of an intelligent designer? So, where does this leave us?

God Is

Reason dictates that we consider some sort of supreme intelligence existing behind the reality surrounding us. Yes, and it also suggests that we return to what is stated about God in the first chapter of Romans: "His eternal power and divine nature, have been clearly seen, being understood through what has been made." Intelligence and purpose of this nature go way beyond the idea of some impersonal force at creation's core. It unquestionably speaks of a being personal in nature—a God who possesses foresight and intentional purpose in bringing these things into existence. Why? We need look no further than ourselves—which of us could create something without intention and the intelligence to do so?

But why the "One God" the Bible so succinctly describes—the God who revealed His name to Moses as "I am that I am?" He told Moses to say to the Israelites *I AM* sent me: *Yahweh* (YHWH) in Hebrew, or *Jehovah* as his name later was rendered. This great monotheistic view held by Israel was dead set against the widespread idol-worship of the day, just as atheism, agnosticism, and the multitude of polytheistic, mystical and animistic religions are in our world today.

God is. This is the reality of God revealed in the Bible. But just what does that mean? Is God just totally big—big enough to create and sustain the kind of universe we've been discussing? Or is he something else, a being of a different nature from what we think of as immense. Is it possible to get our minds wrapped around the idea that he *is*—that predating everything we see before us he and he only exists; has no beginning, no end, that there is no one else? I myself simply can't imagine it! My finite mind is constrained by what I am capable of perceiving as existing in space and time. It is not programmed to envision the infinite. Give this some thought. Do you have the same problem?

But if the self-existent God of the Bible truly is as self-sufficient as he says he is, why would he need to create anything at all? I think the answer lies in a description of his nature: "God is love" as 1 John 4:8 emphatically declares. No, not "love is God" as some hold to be true—*God is love!* If true, would he not also have the desire to express that love in one way or another? Seems logical. Is not the same true for us? Did God *need* this—us? Being self-sufficient, omnipotent and omniscient, he has no needs as we humans know them. Yet the Bible says that he *desires*.

The Bible says…The Bible says…The Bible says! You'll be hearing a lot of that throughout this book. There is, of course, good reason for this. *The Bible says* carries the same weight as *God says*. The Bible, ancient in theme and content, chronicles God's interaction with man from first to last. It not only gives us facts relating to God, but reveals the very nature of God himself. Concerning the Lord Jesus Christ, John 1:1 – 3 states, "In the beginning was the Word, and the Word was with God, and the Word was God. He was in the beginning with God. All things were made through Him, and without Him was not any thing made that was made."

This sheds a whole new light on the subject. But is what the Bible communicates actually true? Is it in fact reliable? Or has its content been corrupted, as many claim, as it has been passed down from generation to generation over thousands of years? I can see why people might be a bit confused—the issue of veracity certainly poses a legitimate question.

Why is the Bible so significant? Because the truth is hidden in its pages, right there before our very eyes, freely accessible to anyone who will search for it. Truth? "Your truth may not be the same as my truth," many claim. They see truth as being relative—that is, it can and does change according to one's circumstances. The Bible, on the other hand, proclaims truth to be absolute. Since God never changes, neither does his truth: "I, the Lord, do not change," declares God the Father in Malachi 3:6. And Hebrews 13:8 states, "Jesus Christ is the same yesterday and today and forever."

As we discussed earlier, the Bible claims that Jesus Christ is the central force behind the existence of the cosmos: "For by Him all things were created, both in the heavens and on earth.… all things have been created through Him and for Him." In John 8:58, Jesus—openly exposing the reality of his nature—unapologetically declares *"I am."* All things were brought into existence through him, and were also created *"for Him."* This is the heart of the matter—unquestionably God's intent for everything we see before us.

It's not too hard, then, to draw the conclusion that mankind, being the zenith of God's created order, possesses a supreme purpose. What is it exactly? Man's very reason for existence is to be united with God—to share eternal life with Him—a theme repeated time and again in the Bible. Jesus is glorified in the full surrender of our lives to him. He really enjoys it!

The Bible claims this all to be true. Yet, doesn't this bring us right back to the question of legitimacy—the very reliability of the Bible itself?

The Bible?

Communication is a funny thing. Think how blown out of proportion news becomes when spread by word of mouth, ever more distorted as it wanders from its original source. There's a game we play that demonstrates this very thing. Put a dozen people in a circle and whisper a brief sentence to the one next to you. Then send it on down the line. By the time the message works its way back to the person who first spoke it, it's been corrupted beyond belief. This, of course, is always good for a laugh, but it also births in us a deep-seated conviction that any communication of this sort can't really be trusted.

People often belittle the reliability of the Bible for the same reason. After all, we're talking here about thousands of years of copying and recopying. But has the Bible actually been passed down to 21st century readers the same way as in the example above? Not at all! First of all, we need to recognize that the content of the Bible consists of written rather than verbal communication. Then we must understand how it has been transferred from generation to generation.

Let's say you traveled to a remote part of the globe where you stumbled upon a very unusual tribe of people, none of whom appeared to be older than forty.

"Where are all the old people?" you ask.

"We are the old people! We don't really keep track but many of us are probably eighty, or even older."

"Did I just discover the fountain of youth?" No, but something very much like it! For centuries the tribe had been concocting a beverage brewed from various herbs, while taken daily obviously preserved their youthful looks. And, surprisingly, the natives were willing to share their secret. You may be wondering what exotic plant could possibly have this effect. Yet the ingredients were not actually at all rare; they could be found in any well-stocked health food store. Quickly grabbing your notebook, you set about recording in precise detail every single ingredient in exact measurement, as well as the temperature and time needed to brew it. "I've got one shot at this. I had better get it right!"

Incredibly, when brewing it up and drinking it as prescribed for a few weeks after arriving home, you actually did appear a bit younger. "I'm so excited! I've got to tell my friends!" Do you suppose they may have wanted the recipe also? That goes without saying! Writing it all down, since computers had not yet come on the scene, they rushed off to try it themselves. And it worked for them just as it had worked for you. This kind of excitement just can't be contained, and soon they each shared it with seven other close friends.

Now, strange as it may seem, after a time you misplaced your own recipe. Horrified, you got right on the phone to each of your four friends, only to find that they also had lost theirs. What to do but contact the other 28 recipients of the formula in hopes of salvaging the recipe for the ingredients of the original. Thankfully, you were able to gather up 26 of the 28 copies.

Now here's the question: what chance do you suppose there was of retrieving the exact formula from those 26 third generation copies? Probably pretty good, don't you think? And that was indeed the case. Twenty of the copies were identically the same—word for word. Three others had one or two misspelled words; two listed an ingredient and measurement out of order, and one added an item not found on any of the others. Given these facts, any reasonable person would have to conclude that the original recipe had truly been preserved.

Scholars call evaluation of historical documents, such as we've just discussed, textual criticism. Through this process they can accurately recreate a document from copies that are centuries removed from its original. All they need is a sufficient supply of material to work from. How much is considered sufficient? As many as possible, of course, but commonly only a few are relied upon. For most ancient compositions not more than a dozen copies exist, and those are often a thousand years older than the originals. By this means we enjoy the literature of antiquity with a high degree of confidence in their accuracy, whether from Greek, Roman, or other ancient cultures.

So, how does the Bible compare? The New Testament was written in Greek, the dominant language of culture and learning of that age. Most people are astounded to learn that biblical scholars have much more material to work from than even the best of any other work of antiquity—beyond five thousand copies, in fact. Not only that, they are much closer in age to the original texts. And if this were not enough, almost the entire New Testament could be reassembled from other ancient writings quoting texts whose originals (known as an autograph) have been lost to history. Moreover, there are accurate translations generated in several other languages as a result of the Gospel being spread from culture to culture. In summary, there is a virtual storehouse of information available for scholars to check and cross-check. These facts remain unchallenged in academic circles.

As one might expect, there are numerous variations amongst all the available documents. Yet the vast majority of these differences are inconsequential: spelling errors, inverted phrases, and even a few additions and deletions not found in the majority of the texts. Of the 20,000 lines of the New Testament only 40 are questionable, and none of them challenge any major doctrine of the Christian faith. Reliable? No question about it![1]

Well, that's the story of the Bible's New Testament, but what about the Old Testament? Actually, it's the same. The evidence? In 1946 some Bedouin shepherds found ancient scrolls preserved in clay jars in the Qumran caves above the Dead Sea

---

[1]   See: The Path through the Maze, by the author, pgs. 14 – 18

in Israel. Over the course of the next ten years some 100,000 scrolls and fragments were discovered. The most notable of these is a complete copy of the Book of Isaiah dating back to around 200 B.C.

What's truly remarkable is the fact that this duplicate is virtually identical to today's Masoretic text of Isaiah commonly used by Jews today. This is the text from which our present translation of the Old Testament comes. Jewish scribes have meticulously preserved the integrity of these scriptures down through four millennia, starting with what came from the hand of Moses himself.

The historical facts surrounding the preservation of the Bible are fascinating, aren't they. But what is even more intriguing is the message of its pages—that is, what God has revealed about himself to everyone who "has ears to hear!"

Revelation

When people think of the concept of revelation in regard to Scripture, their minds typically go to the book of the Bible bearing that name. But while the Book of Revelation indeed prophesies events which are to take place in the future, and therefore is often somewhat overemphasized by some who study the Bible, it actually takes a backseat to the sweeping truth Scripture puts forth.

You see, the entire Bible is a book of revelation. The Bible's chief purpose is not merely to communicate knowledge about God in order that we might gain a reasonable understanding of his intervention into the affairs of humanity. Its content contains immeasurably more than knowing about God; it expresses the fact that he has given us the opportunity, the ability, and the privilege of knowing him on a personal level. Yes, Person to person! When the Bible says that we have been created in God's image, it conveys the reality that God himself is a person, one whom we can get to know personally. It follows, then, that we have been privileged with the capability and predisposition to pursue the kind of relationship with him he meant for us to experience. This is the purpose for which we were created!

Communicating his intentions in this very practical way obviously boils down to his intervention in our lives for the purpose of drawing us to him. God primarily reveals himself to us today by sharing what he has done down through history with those who have experienced his touch—and why he has done it. The Bible is the written record of what he has done in the multitude of human lives, revealing the fact that he intends to reach into your life the same way also. It says in Romans 15:4, "For whatever was written in former days was written for our instruction, that through endurance and through the encouragement of the Scriptures we might have hope."

As was emphasized when we began this discussion, we must focus on the question of purpose—though not our own purpose, but God's. We shouldn't be surprised to find that this truth flies in the face of the egocentric view we have of ourselves. After all, which of us has not dwelt on the thought, "I wish I knew what the purpose of my life is; I just don't understand." I've encountered this confusion time and again in believers, whether they be new or more seasoned in their faith. There's no need to beat ourselves up over this issue, because we find it quite common to the whole of mankind. Bewilderment about our purpose in life is indeed the underlying basis of philosophical thought down through history. But shouldn't all those philosophers have figured this whole thing out by now? Should they not have come to a common consensus of truth? Obviously, this is not the case!

Everything revolves around the fact that God has a purpose for this fine-tuned universe which we—as the apex of his created order—are privileged to inhabit. What exactly is this all-embracing truth the Bible presents, and how can we come to know it? One might sum up its purpose this way: Life on Earth is sort of an incubator, a temporary place of testing wherein the children of God ultimately rise to the surface as His chosen ones, eventually hatching for the purpose of serving and glorifying him.

Still, a huge roadblock stands in the way of fully grasping God's purpose for us. The problem lies with the use of the term "my." When we ignore the fact that God himself is the one responsible for creating me with purpose—*his* purpose—"my" life always becomes a stumbling-block in our own mind. And even when we come to better terms with the idea, it can still be confusing. Why? Because we tend to equate God's purpose with doing rather than being. It always seems to be what I have been created to *do* as opposed to what have I been created to *be*. The Bible contains the answers to all our questions. But we must look closely, not simply reading its content, but carefully studying it.

God is calling each one of us unto himself. Whether you realize it or not, he has been doing so throughout the course of your life. There comes a time for each of us when that call—that revelation— becomes more and more clear and personal. There comes a time when God's expectation comes to the forefront. There comes a time when we are not just invited, but obligated to believe.

Faith

Revelation about God springs from his desire, and therefore his intention, to show himself to us. What an awesome privilege it is! Even so, why doesn't he do it in a manner more familiar to us—through our physical senses? Why not reveal himself so that we can see with our eyes, hear with our ears, touch, smell or even taste him? Actually, he did in fact do just that by sending Jesus to live among us—God and man in the same person. What was the result of this visitation? The biblical record shows that many believed but many others refused to do so, even when presented with the hard evidence of his many miracles.

An interesting example of this phenomenon is found in John 20:24 – 29 concerning one of Christ's disciples. After his death and resurrection, the other disciples told Thomas they had indeed seen Jesus. But he refused to believe that he had been raised from the dead saying, "Unless I see in his hands the mark of the nails, and place my finger into the mark of the nails, and place my hand into his side, I will never believe." Considering the fact that this all came after spending three years at Jesus' side while he performed astounding signs, his behavior seems a bit dumbfounding. Yet Jesus accommodated the weakness of his unbelief by personally appearing to him, wherein Thomas exclaimed, "My Lord and my God!" Jesus responded, "Have you believed because you have seen me? Blessed are those who have not seen and yet have believed."

Well, as substantiating as the evidence found in the Gospels truly is, it did take place a long, long time ago. Jesus obviously is not physically with us today, yet he still requires that we believe. There is good reason for this: "Without faith it is impossible to please him, for whoever would draw near to God must believe that he exists and that he rewards those who seek him," as chapter 11 of the Book of Hebrews emphatically declares.

Have you thought about the fact that from the very beginning of God's interaction with man he required faith as the touchstone of relationship with him? After centuries of God's personal involvement with their forefathers, the Israelites spent over four hundred years in Egypt, first as guests and then as slaves. Then came God in majestic power, wondrously releasing them from their bondage and leading them to the land of promise first guaranteed to Abraham. This all came about through a series of astounding miracles—God proving himself to them. And yet when God hid his presence once again, they almost immediately fell short of believing him. They failed to believe that he was faithful—capable, even—to bring about what he had promised. The Old Testament is a record not only of the promises and rewards of faith, but also a testimony to the devastating consequences of unbelief.

Why do people choose to reject what God is so clearly calling them to, instead relying only on what they are able to see? In Israel's case it was false idols made of wood or stone often overlayed with gold, as well as what they observed in the heavens—sun, moon, and a sky littered with stars. The relevant point here is "seeing." Seeing certainly takes a whole lot less effort than merely relying on what one has been told. So it has been down through the millennia until today. Man prefers to put his faith in what he can physically experience rather than trusting in a God he can't, whether it be idols of gold or the god of self-reliance.

Christians are often accused of having "blind faith." Not so! Our faith is rooted in the viable evidence of both God's existence and his will for our lives, just as we have been discussing. A comical but sad commentary on those who make such a charge is that they themselves are the culprits of their accusations. Having no deeper thought about the afterlife than poking a little fun, a popular saying a while back went like this: "I'm going to the place that's fluffy, not stuffy." Talk about blind faith!

What is faith? Hebrews 11 says, "Faith is the assurance of things hoped for, the conviction [*evidence*] of things not seen." *Assurance* and *conviction* are absolutely essential to the experience both of the initiation of faith and its growth as a believer matures. So, it's not surprising that we hear so much said about them. But faith has no possibility of even existing unless *"things hoped for"* is first there. Why would we hope for something we don't care about? The same holds true for *"things not seen"* because there's no need for faith when something can be perceived through our natural senses.[2]

The Bible uses two different words—*faith* and *believe*. Are faith and believing one and the same? Yes, they both are translated from the same root word in the original language, Greek— faith as a noun and believe as a verb. So, why not simply use belief to describe both? Maybe the answer lies in the fact that faith consists of something deeper, the kind of belief proven by action—that is, the manner in which we choose to live our lives. The Bible talks about the "obedience of faith"—*obedience* being the evidence that faith truly exists. Unquestionably, faith in God must be walked-out over the course of a lifetime. Faith is both a gift from God and an act of our will.

---

[2] See: *Free from the Power of Sin* by the author, pages 84 – 87

Truth

What we believe is the most powerful motivating force in human existence. Our behavior is a true reflection of what we believe. Just try to shake a person loose from what he has come to accept as a deep-seated belief. Though not impossible, it can be very difficult. Changing one's mind often takes being presented with verifiable facts. In the case of spiritual beliefs—the truth of the Gospel—it takes a touch from God himself: "No one can come to me unless the Father who sent me draws him," Jesus responded to those who were dumbfounded over his claim of having come down from heaven, all captured in detail in the Gospel of John, chapter 6.

What you believe matters—you are staking your life on it! Jesus made a startling pronouncement in his Sermon on the Mount found in the sixth chapter of Matthew: "The eye is the lamp of the body. So, if your eye is healthy your whole body will be full of light, but if your eye is bad, your whole body will be full of darkness. If then the light in you is darkness, how great is the darkness!" Though this teaching seems a bit mysterious, its meaning is actually quite simple. Your eye means perception. If you properly perceive God's reality, you will be filled with the light of his truth. If you fail to comprehend God's truth, you will find yourself overcome by the darkness of deceit. And there is another essential ingredient of this teaching: If you believe a lie relating to God's nature and purpose—if you are convinced that you are on the right path, yet wrong—it will be very difficult to be convinced otherwise. It is not uncommon for people to fall into the hopelessness of deceit from which it is not easy to escape.

You are betting your life on what you believe in your heart! This has been true since ancient times. Moses confirmed this principle in Deuteronomy 30:19 – 20:

> "I call heaven and earth to witness against you today, that I have set before life and death, blessing and curse. Therefore choose life, that you and your offspring may live, loving the Lord your God, obeying his voice and holding fast to him, for he is your life and length of days…"

This is why it is critical that we understand the Gospel (meaning *Good News!*) of Jesus Christ. What exactly is this Good News? Here's how the apostle Paul succinctly explains it in 1 Corinthians 15:1 – 4:

> "Now I would remind you, brothers, of the gospel I preached to you, which you received, in which you stand, and by which you are being saved, if you hold fast to the word I preached to you— unless you believed in vain. For I delivered to you as of first importance what I also received: that Christ died for our sins in accordance with the Scriptures, that he was buried, that he was raised on the third day in accordance with the Scriptures."

And Paul goes one step further. In Galatians 1:8 – 12, he warns against distorting Christ's gospel:

> "But even if we or an angel from heaven should preach to you a gospel contrary to the one we preached to you, let him be accursed…For I would have you know, brothers, that the gospel

that was preached by me is not man's gospel. For
I did not receive it from any man, nor was I taught
it, but I received it through a revelation of Jesus
Christ."

Why so harsh? Because the truth of the Gospel does not
come from man but from God himself! It is God's personal revelation to mankind and therefore not to be taken lightly, or worse,
ignored.

It is important to note that Paul's epistles (letters) comprise
half of the books of the New Testament. Their content is rich
and vital to understand. His writings bring to light not just the
fact but the *meaning* of Christ's coming. They entail the plan
of salvation along with its declarations, promises and doctrines.
Paul explains who Jesus is and what he came to do. It is the
"Good News" defined. Truth, you ask? It's all there in black and
white—the heart of the gospel just waiting to be discovered.[3]

---

[3]   See: *Free from the Power of Sin,* by the author, Pgs. 8 – 13

Judgment

Consider what Jesus taught in his Sermon on the Mount found in Matthew 7:13 – 14: "Enter by the narrow gate. For the gate is wide and the way is easy that leads to destruction, and those who enter by it are many. For the gate is narrow and the way is hard that leads to life, and those who find it are few." After testifying to this, Jesus devotes the rest of his sermon to a further explanation of both his promise and the warning that accompanies it. Most striking about this disturbing passage is what is found in verses 21 – 23. To those who were pretty sure that their good works and exceptional giftings would save them, Jesus makes this gut-wrenching statement, "And then I will declare to them, 'I never knew you; depart from me, you workers of lawlessness.'"

What, then, is the criteria for being allowed to enter the kingdom of heaven? As written in verses 24 – 27, knowing and pleasing God through our obedience to him is the key: "Everyone who hears these words of mine and does them will be like a wise man who built his house on the rock"—a structural foundation unassailable not only by the storms of life but also by the fiery darts of deceit and accusation continually thrown by the evil one.

How can we know that our walk with Jesus will be fruitful? Examining our motives is essential. Is my life centered on God and his purpose, or am I living for myself? For those who are practicing a rebellious and sinful lifestyle the difference is obvious. But it's a bit more complicated for those hoping that their good works will save them. Yet knowing whether your life is focused on Christ or deceptively wrapped up in yourself is actually quite simple, because the Holy Spirit within will to let you know. 2 Corinthians 13:5 tells us, "Examine yourselves, to see whether you are in the faith. Test yourselves. Or do you not realize this about yourselves, that Jesus Christ is in you?—unless indeed you fail to meet the test!"

Jesus promised that he would come back to us again. And when he does, he will come with power. The Book of Revelation, chapter 19:11 – 16, describes his second coming. And the very next chapter portrays Jesus sitting on a great white throne, all humanity standing in judgment before him. He holds a book—the *Book of Life.* Anyone whose name is not found written in this book is to be thrown into the lake of fire. Sobering, to say the least; terrifying if you stop to really think about it. Judgment is on the way; your life is being held in the balance as we speak.

The Bible speaks repeatedly of the consequence of how we live our lives here on earth. Throughout the Gospels Jesus warned of hell, of being cast "into the outer darkness where there will be weeping and the gnashing of teeth." Both the Old and New Testaments talk about the eventual destruction of the ungodly. Philippians 3:18 – 19 says:

> For many, of whom I have often told you and now tell even with tears, walk as enemies of the cross of Christ. Their end is destruction, their god is their belly, and their glory is in their shame, with minds set on earthly things.

And yet, in spite of all this foretold misery, God has an eternal purpose. Paul tells us in Romans 9:22 – 23:

> What if God, desiring to show his wrath and to make and to make known his power, has endured with much patience vessels of wrath prepared for destruction, in order to make known the riches of his glory for vessels of mercy, which he has prepared beforehand for glory.

Stemming from our earnest desire to see people surrender their lives to Christ, the harsh message of avoiding hell often becomes a prominent theme in our witness to others. The fear it is meant to produce can indeed be quite an "eye-opener," as well it should be. But even more important is the awful outcome of missing God's purpose for my life. Just imagine people, after receiving their final judgment, trudging off to eternal separation from their Creator—those to whom so much hope was planned; those who have come to realize how monumental the stakes truly are.

Hebrews 9:27 warns, "It is appointed for man to die once, and after that comes judgment." For those who believe these are not grounds for fear, but of hope, all resulting from choices that have been laid before us: CHOICES! It has been said that in this world God gives us enough light to find our way to him, and yet leaves enough darkness to stumble around and be lost forever. Choose life!

Called

Consider the fact that we live in a world governed by laws—mostly good, some bad. These laws administer what is known as a "World Order," which has assumed its place as dominant in the affairs of mankind. This *order* is self-perpetuating. Generation to generation education trains those who are destined to take their rightful place in its service. Sounds a bit nefarious, doesn't it? Not necessarily; we must have order to survive. The power this world order bestows on its participants, however, often consumes them. The destructive influence of Satan is at the core of much of this worldwide power struggle.

Are we then to shun this powerful system—this *kingdom*, of sorts? Is it wrong to want to achieve success in our careers and businesses? Is desiring to build a meaningful life here on earth sinful? How could it be when we have been created with an innate desire to build families and the need to provide for both them and ourselves. Despite the corrupting power that often results from man's greed, God has initiated the establishment of institutions so profoundly significant for our lives. And he means to support this system—even abundantly bless our participation in it! We shouldn't be ashamed over what we desire to accomplish on this earth. On the other hand, we must keep our priorities straight.

You see, God's kingdom existed long before man was allowed to create his own. His is an eternal kingdom ruled by the Lord Jesus Christ himself. Pilate, who only understood raw power but not the very nature of truth itself, asked Jesus if he really was a king. He responded, "My kingdom is not of this world." God's order—his rule—takes precedence over anything the world has to offer. And what's wonderful is that we as his children are invited to share in it all. We have been *called* to this lofty and privileged position!

This strikes at the very core of God' s purpose. He has created a people for his own possession, a people who willingly surrender their lives, their entire being, to him. Nothing less suffices; his kingdom is one populated by those called to be his children. It's what our worldly existence is all about.

The question is, just who are being called? All of us, it seems. The Bible is very clear about this: 1 John 2:2 says that Jesus died, "not for our sins only, but also for the sins of the whole world." That is, he sacrificed his own life to save every person who ever lived. "Opportunity knocks," as the saying goes; his awesome promise has been extended to the entire world.

But in order to appreciate this opportunity for what it truly is, we must be "born again," as Jesus said in John 3:3: "Truly, Truly, I say to you, unless one is born again he cannot see the kingdom of God." You cannot enter God's kingdom, nor can you even begin to understand it unless you have been born again. This strange term refers to a radical conversion—that is, a shifting from one form to another. "Therefore, if anyone is in Christ, he is a new creation. The old has passed away; behold, the new has come," as it says in 2 Corinthians 5:17. After his conversion to Christianity, the 18th century British slave ship captain John Newton abandoned his profession and wrote the iconic hymn *Amazing Grace*: "I once was lost but now am found, was blind but now I see."

Our nature is comprised of body, soul and spirit—our spirit being most essential since through it, God communicates and communes with us. But man's spirit, once alive to God, has suffered death because of sin. It is only "awakened" as we fully surrender to God and his purpose for our life.[4]

Many say, "I tried reading the Bible, but stopped because I just don't understand it." No wonder; the Bible bears the stamp

---

[4]   See *Free from the Power of Sin,* by the author. Pgs. 33 - 36

of divine inspiration—it's simply impossible to comprehend without illumination from the Spirit of God. Through Christ's revelation, however, even the simplest—the least sophisticated—people on earth can understand the Good News of God's kingdom. It's for everyone!

Becoming a child of God begins with a call. "But how can I receive this call?" Interestingly, every time you hear the truth about God—his Gospel—no matter how brief it might be, you are being called to him. Paul brings this all into perspective in the tenth chapter of the Book of Romans: "So faith comes from hearing, and hearing through the word of Christ [or, *concerning* Christ]." Hearing the truth is how Jesus first attracts people to himself, and then leads them to believe. Romans 10 goes on to say, "Everyone who believes in him will not be put to shame" and, "Everyone who calls on the name of the Lord will be saved." God's drawing people to himself, and then helping them to believe, can only happen through the gift of his abundant grace.

Those who have "found" God have come to this awareness not merely by gathering a set of facts. Rather, God has "found" them. Their knowledge of God is the result of revelation, not solely from investigation. Yes, he will begin to draw those who merely seek biblical knowledge, but coming to actually know Him is ultimately His doing, not ours. It is not primarily a matter of inviting Jesus into our life, although there certainly is a meaningful element to that. Rather, he is inviting us into his.[5] Galatians 4:9 says it well, "But now that you have come to know God, or rather to be known by God…" And in Revelation 3:20, Jesus promises:

> Behold, I stand at the door and knock. If anyone
> hears my voice and opens the door, I will come in
> to him and eat with him, and he with me.

---

5 See: *There is a River,* by the author, Pg. 12

There really is no excuse for not knowing. "I just didn't know" may fly with people who've never heard the Good News, but not for those dwelling in a land teeming with churches, Bibles and various Christian media. Yes, we've heard; we are continually being presented with God's offer. Indeed, you are being called right now as you read this book! Should not his invitation, then, at the very least merit further investigation? Romans chapter 10—study it; believe it! It has been written for you:

> If you confess with your mouth that Jesus is Lord and believe in your heart that God raised him from the dead, you will be saved. For with the heart one believes and is justified, and with the mouth one confesses and is saved. Romans 10:9 - 10

The Bible is authoritative—a book rich in promises, but also one full of warnings. The declaration Jesus made in Matthew 22:14 is among the most blunt: "For many are called [or, *invited*], but few are chosen."

Chosen

Many are called, but few are chosen. "I think I now see what calling is all about, but what does it mean to be *chosen* by God?" Going back to what we discussed in chapter 7, God has given us the opportunity, the ability, and the honor of knowing him on a personal level. When the Bible says that we have been created in God's image, it conveys the reality that God himself is a person, and as such, one whom we can personally get to know. It follows, then, that we have been privileged with both the capability and predisposition to pursue the kind of relationship with him he means for us to experience—the purpose for which we were created. Paul goes even further in Romans 8:28 – 29:

> And we know that for those who love God all things work together for good, for those who are called according to his purpose. For those whom he foreknew he also predestined to be conformed to the image of his Son, in order that he might be the firstborn among many brothers.

Chosen to uniquely share eternal life with God, while all others are banished from him forever? Is it possible to overemphasize such a privilege? Hardly! But the question remains, who are these chosen ones, and why have they been selected for such honor? God reveals who they are in the first chapter of John's Gospel, verses 9 – 13:

> The true light, which gives light to everyone, was coming into the world. He was in the world, and the world was made through him, yet the world did not know him. He came to his own, and his

> own people did not receive him. But to all who
> did receive him, who believed in his name, he
> gave the right to become children of God, who
> were born not of blood nor of the will of the flesh
> nor of the will of man, but of God.

In attempting to understand this, it is helpful—utterly essential, really—to know that God is selective in his choice of those who will ultimately rise to top as his beloved ones, his children. To become a child of God he merely asks that we believe in him and then demonstrate that belief by committing to a life of surrender and obedience. Simple? Yes. Easy? No!

When asked what is the greatest commandment in God's Law, Jesus replied, "You shall love the Lord your God with all your heart and with all your soul and with all your mind. This is the great and first commandment." Now, I don't know about you but I find this hard to wrap my mind around. How is it possible for any mortal being to comprehend the magnitude of this teaching, much less hope to fulfill it? Obviously, it can only happen by the grace of God, and with the help of the Holy Spirit. There are indeed many examples of such zealous devotion found among God's people throughout the Bible. But what about me? I love God a lot—but to that extent?

Yet I find it interesting that there are examples of this kind of love right here on earth, even among those who do not even live for God. I'm speaking of the human penchant to fall in love. Do we even know how this "falling in love" happens between people—this giving of our heart to another? The passion of that first infatuation eventually simmers down, but if allowed to grow, those in love desire to be together sharing an intimacy lasting a lifetime. Is this not much like what we see at the heart of Jesus' teaching about loving God, committing to Him with every fiber of our being through thick and thin, for better or for worse? The weakness in this comparison is, of course, that an earthly love relationship is merely temporal while, for a life surrendered to God, love takes on eternal significance.

The last twelve verses of Ephesians chapter 5 speak of the union between husband and wife, and with it a corresponding relationship linking God and his people. It talks about commitment and the bond between the partners, comparing the two situations with one another. Verses 31 and 32 sum it up this way:

> Therefore a man shall leave his father and mother and hold fast to his wife, and the two shall become one flesh. This mystery is profound, and I am saying that it refers to Christ and the church.

Hard to understand? Not really. Believe in God's promise, surrender your life to Jesus as Lord and Savior, acknowledge and turn away from your sin, commit your life in faithfulness to him, and you will find this truth, his purpose for you, quickly coming to fruition in your life.

Whether you are convinced that Christians have been specially elected by God for an unalterable bond with him before time began, or you believe that through God's gift of free will you possess the choice to freely receive him and thus become his child, the fact remains that in God's inexplicable foreknowledge he knows who are his own.

Just what does God's foreknowledge actually mean? Is it simply knowing who belong to him in advance, or is something much deeper, something beyond our comprehension? The debate in trying to determine, and then establish doctrine concerning it all has been going on for centuries. Isn't it time we override our personal interpretations? Why not simply accept the reality of his great love as depicted by Paul in Romans 11:33: "Oh, the depth of the riches both of the wisdom and knowledge of God! How unsearchable are his judgments and unfathomable his ways!"

Of utmost importance is that we walk out our lives in a manner worthy of him. 2 Peter 1:10 says, "Therefore, brothers, be all the more diligent to confirm your calling and election, for if you practice these qualities you will never fall." Scripture tells us time and again that we have a part to play in this story. God never changes. He will always be faithful to us; we must also remain faithful to him. The Book of Hebrews exhorts us in verse 3:14: "For we have come to share in Christ, if indeed we hold our original confidence firm to the end."

Because we are human, we will stumble. Yet there's no need to fall. It's why we need to drive in the stake of our commitment—drive it deep—unshakable and holding fast for whatever comes our way. God is trustworthy. He promises you peace and strength for the battle ahead. Help is always on the way!

We've now reached a critical point in our narrative!
The following will be of benefit only if you have given your
life to Christ and desire to grow in your walk with God.

Intimacy

God wants you! He wants all of you! This is the overarching truth found throughout the pages of the Bible. He will settle for nothing less. And why should he? If he did in fact fashion you for the very purpose of joining you to himself eternally, he ought to be entitled to your entire being here and now!

You have been shaped by a formidable God, one who is all-knowing and all-powerful, and capable of sustaining a universe so vast that even our most powerful telescopes cannot grasp its immensity. The question is, why you? Why would God create *you* for such purpose? Ephesians 1:4 talks about your being in the mind of God before the foundation of the earth was laid, and then being intimately conceived. Psalm 139 describes this truth in stunning detail, ending with, "Your eyes saw my unformed substance; in your book were written, every one of them, the days that were formed for me, when as yet there was none of them."

If this does not characterize the uniqueness of your individuality, I don't know what could! Cherished, beloved, significant—*priceless*, really. And this portrayal merely scratches the surface of your meaning to God. He wants nothing less than all of you! He has designed you as his own possession, as it so clearly declares in 1 Corinthians 6:19 – 20:

"Do you not know that your body is a temple of the Holy Spirit within you, whom you have from God? You are not your own, for you were bought with a price. So glorify God in your body."

"I am a jealous God," he unapologetically asserts in many places, meaning he refuses to let you share yourself with another. Selfish? No, merely bringing a sense of reality to our situation, as he affirms in Isaiah 43:1, "I have called you by name, you are mine."

In the end, it's not about where God is at in my life, but where I am at in his! And this brings us to the subject of *intimacy*. What does Jesus want from us? What is his foremost desire?

Once we are saved, we are called to a path of spiritual growth—not as an option but as a necessity. God has created us for an eternal destiny, and therefore has a specific plan for our life. To truly discover His plan, our pursuit of the gospel must be a way of life. Yet being human, we naturally tend toward superficiality as we go about our daily lives. Truth be told, it's far more comfortable—so much less demanding—than pursuing intimate relationship with God. Our self-centered nature would much rather be involved with Christ as some sort of addition to our life, leaning on Him only when we have needs.[6]

It's no wonder we feel a void in our walk with God. Many Christians are perfectly content with attending a weekly church service, joining in singing a few worship songs, appreciating a good sermon, and enjoying fellowship with friends. They may even attend a midweek home group or Bible study. There is obviously nothing wrong with these activities and we are instructed to pursue them: "Let us consider how to stir up one another to love and good works, not neglecting to meet together, as is the habit of some, but encouraging one another," as it says in Hebrews 10:24 – 25. But surprisingly, these activities can also

---

[6]   See: *There is a River* by the author, pg. 43

lead to a sense of emptiness. This is because God has designed us for more, much more.

Personal interaction is at the heart of God's desire for our life in him, a life built on deep affection and connection. But just how does that all work, you might ask. How is it practical, or even possible? To begin with, can you imagine *any* relationship being cultivated devoid of spending time together? Out of the question, isn't it? So it is with God. Intimacy with Jesus—getting to truly know him—stems from time spent with him.

Have you wondered why it is so difficult to carve out a portion of your day to quietly meet with God? It seems almost impossible, doesn't it? As we get our day started, we'd rather do almost anything other than slow down and take time to seek God. But since Jesus invites you into such extraordinary communion with himself, it seems unreasonable that we would choose to refuse it. And yet we do! How can we go about changing this tendency in our nature? It's not so much a matter of changing as it is being changed! We must give God the time it takes to mold us. Demanding, yes, but it can soon grow into a delight. As we begin to step into this spiritual discipline, our appetite for greater intimacy is instinctively kindled. Why? Because nothing in life compares to sensing his voice, of receiving a personal touch from God.

You have been presented with a crucial part to play in this story—the duty of setting the stage for intimacy. You do this by opening yourself up to Jesus. Admittedly, pursuing such affection with one we cannot see can be a bit challenging. Yet not hopeless! Ephesians 6:18 tells us to, "Pray at all times in the Spirit, with all prayer and supplication." Pray, seek, ask—not just about your needs, or interceding for others, but for God's touch. Ask for his presence to envelop you. And then be willing to listen. Quieting yourself enough to hear that inward voice is a skill worth developing as Jesus provides the grace to do so.

You will find prayer less of an effort when blended with reading your Bible. The written Word of God is obviously a must if you are to better understand and appreciate Jesus, for in its pages resides the fullness of his revelation concerning himself and his purpose for your life. Combined with prayer, it becomes more than simply reading. God intends for you to experience the magnitude of his being as you study his Word. In it we find horizons we may never have imagined to exist—the full counsel of God.

And take it a step further. Spend the time and effort needed to memorize passages from the Bible. Yes, it's a tall order—one of the most demanding spiritual disciplines you will encounter—yet totally worth it. This is something you can work on throughout your day, helping to focus your thoughts on Jesus as you do life. Reciting Scripture during your quiet time, and as a result meaningfully meditating on what has been hidden deep within, automatically cultivates a remarkable level of revelation.

Look for spiritual giftings from God. Paul tells us in Ephesians 4:7, "Grace was given to each one of us according to the measure of Christ's gift." Explore the gifts portrayed in 1 Corinthians 12 and Romans 12. I'd like to be able to tell you exactly what to expect from intimacy with Jesus, but each of us is unique, and he deals with us individually. I can tell you one thing: it will be marvelous. Yes, there will be times when things seem a bit dry. But then, often unexpectedly, the Holy Spirit will explode into your heart and you will never be the same.

* * * * *

Finally, we need to explore a further reason God has provided for such intimacy between you and himself: service to him and his kingdom. Scripture is very clear that the Spirit of God wants you working alongside him as he reaches into this hurting world to save and provide for those in need—which, by the way, means all of us in one way or another:

> To equip the saints for the work of ministry, for building up the body of Christ, until we all attain to the unity of the faith and of the knowledge of the Son of God, to mature manhood, to the measure of the stature of the fullness of Christ.
> Ephesians 4:12 – 13

Service to God doesn't seem like such a chore when you realize it is Jesus calling you—that he has a specific and individual purpose for your life. There's not a job too big or too small that he cannot use you as he sees fit. And the beauty of it is that he has already trailblazed the path he wants you to take. He says so in Ephesians 2:10: "For we are his workmanship, created in Christ Jesus for good works, which God prepared beforehand, that we should walk in them."

Recognize what Christ Jesus the Lord has done in saving you! "His divine power has granted to us all things that pertain to life and godliness, through the knowledge of him who called us to his own glory and excellence," as he boldly reveals through his trusted servant in 2 Peter 1:3. Do you want to experience the joy of the Lord and the gifts of the Holy Spirit? Serve as he calls! Pursue him, seeking his inspiration and guidance just as the apostle Paul invoked in his profound and timeless prayer for the Church found in Ephesians 3:16 - 21:

> That according to the riches of his glory he may grant you to be strengthened with power through his Spirit in your inner being, so that Christ may dwell in your hearts through faith—that you, being rooted and grounded in love, may have strength to comprehend with all the saints what is

the breadth and length and height and depth, and
to know the love of Christ that surpasses knowledge, that you may filled up with all the fullness
of God.

Now to him who is able to do far more
abundantly than all we ask or think, according to
the power at work within us, to him be the glory
in the church and in Christ Jesus throughout all
generations, forever and ever. Amen.

Now may the God of hope fill you with all joy
and peace in believing, so that you will abound
in hope by the power of the Holy Spirit.

Romans 15:13